Plays for
Young Actors

Beatrice Holloway

TSL Drama

First published in Great Britain in 2019
By TSL Publications, Rickmansworth

Copyright © 2019 Beatrice Holloway

ISBN / 978-1-912416-79-0

Cover image: https://pixabay.com/en/drama-comedy-and-tragedy-theater-312318/

Rights of performance

Dedication

so many, alongside the performers,
to thank for such marvellous entertainment.

Contents

for five year olds

Mouse Mansion

Characters

Mother Mouse — Teacher
Father Mouse — Teacher
Mouse 1 — young person
Mouse 2 — young person
Mouse 3 — young person
Mouse 4 — young person
Mouse 5 — young person
Mouse 6 — young person
Mouse 7 — young person
Mouse 8 — young person
Four Paws — young person
Two Legs — young person

Running Time

15 minutes

Setting

Scene 1 Confined space behind skirting of sitting room

Scene 2 Sitting room with door off to kitchen

Scene 3 Confined space behind skirting of sitting room

Scene 1

The mouse family has just moved into a new home. The children are squeaking and scampering about excitedly. Once or twice Four Paws prowls around the edge of the stage and Two Legs can be heard humming a tune.

Mother Mouse: Our new house is so roomy. It's called a mansion and belongs to Two legs.

Father Mouse: We need some things to complete it, make it a real home for the children.

Mother M: I shall send them into the big house so they can find one or two useful things.

Father M: Good idea, Go on children, off you go.

(*The children rush for the door, chattering and laughing.*)

Mouse 1: (*Tumbling over in excitement.*) We're going on an adventure.

Mother M: (*Screaming.*) Stop, stop. We forgot to tell you about Four Paws.

Mouse 2: Four Paws? Who is Four Paws?

Father M: He is very big and hairy and he can harm you.

Mouse 3: Will he eat me?

Father M: Bless you no, but he is so clumsy.

Mother M: He will throw you up in the air, he thinks you like it.

Mouse 4: Sound like play fun to me.

Father M: Off you go, and remember stay away from Four Paws.

(Slowly not too sure now and looking a little scared, the children leave.)

Scene 2

The little mice scamper about, giggling and feeling safe as Four Paws is not around. Suddenly Four Paws stalks into the room, head up in a stalking stance.

Four Paws: *(Slyly in an exaggerated friendly voice.)* Hello children. Where are you? *(Mice hide and some begin to shake.)* Meow. Please come and play with me. *(The children quietly shake their heads.)*

Mouse 5:   I want to go home.

Mouse 6:   Shush, Four Paws will hear you.

Four Paws: I know you're there somewhere. Please play, I'm so lonely. Meow. Meow. *(The mice shake and keep quiet. Then they hear a spoon being tapped on a plate.)*

Two Legs: Come on pussy cat, time for your dinner. It's your favourite salmon today.

Four Paws: Oh bother, I want to play with those little mice but I'm so hungry I think I'll have my dinner first. *(Two Legs comes in off stage.)*

Two Legs: There you are. *(Four Paws walks round and round her then rolls onto his back and Two legs strokes his tummy.)* Come on cheeky. I know all about your cupboard love. *(She walks out and Four Paws, head up proudly follows her.)*

Mouse 5:   *(Wails.)* I want to go home

Mouse 7:   So do I. I was very afraid he was going to catch me.

Mouse 8:	Well, he's gone now, and I'm getting hungry, so let's go.
Mouse 1:	I'm glad he's gone. I think he might have eaten one of us, he said he was hungry. (*He holds out his hands and they all dance in a circle singing together.*)
All Children:	Four Paws, Four Paws, Goodbye now. We'd rather play with a farmer's cow, who gently moos, and not meows.
	(*They leave the stage.*)

Scene 3
OR play could stand on its own.

Father M:	The children have been gone a long time. Do you think they are all right?
Mother M:	I think ... (*The mice rush in scampering all about and squeaking excitedly.*) Here they are at last.
	(*All the children crowd round their parents, trying to tell them what they had found and how they met up with Four Paws.*)
Father:	Wow! One at a time please. (*Turns to Mouse 2.*) Now tell me what did you find?
Mouse 2:	Look! (*Holds up a ladies handkerchief.*) This will make a lovely bedspread for my bed.
Mother M:	That's a lovely idea. Now what have you got Mouse 3?
Mouse 3:	Feel this. (*Holds out a cotton wool ball.*) I thought we could all have really soft pillows. (*Strokes her face with a cotton ball and sighs.*)

Father M:	Just what I've always wanted. What's that you've got my little mouse 4?
Mouse 4:	(*Holds up a shiny piece of silver foil.*) I thought it would make a lovely mirror.
Mother M:	Everyone could have their own mirror. (*Mice nod, then fidget and begin washing their faces with their paws.*)
Mouse 6:	(*Very dramatically all the mice are still and solemn.*) We saw Four Paws.
Mouse 7:	He likes to eat salmon, so it's true he won't eat mice.
Mouse 5:	But I was very afraid. He is so big and I think he tells fibs.
Mouse 6:	He wanted to play, but we stayed very very quiet and couldn't find us.
Mother M:	Oh my children! (*She cries into her apron.*) If he had caught you well, we would never see you again. (*The children laugh, go to her and cuddle her then...*)
Mouse 8:	We made up a song about Four Paws.
Mouse 7:	We shall sing it you if you like. (*They get into a circle and sing the song.*)
All Children:	Four Paws, Four Paws, Goodbye now. We'd rather play with a farmer's cow who gently moos, and not meows.
	(*Parent mice clap.*)
Father M:	Well done all of you, I'm very proud of you.

for five year olds

Mice at Play

Characters

Mother Mouse — Teacher
Father Mouse — Teacher
Mouse 1 — young person
Mouse 2 — young person
Mouse 3 — young person
Mouse 4 — young person
Mouse 5 — young person
Mouse 6 — young person
Mouse 7 — young person
Mouse 8 — young person

Running Time

20 minutes

Setting

A sitting room

Inside Mouse Mansion. Throughout the play, the mice should be fidgety, cleaning themselves, exploring etc if they are not speaking.

Mother Mouse: The children have been out playing for a long time Father Mouse.

Father Mouse: I expect they are having fun and forgotten the time.

Mother Mouse: Go and call them in for me, it's time they were in bed.

(*Father M. leaves and is heard off stage calling the children. They all scamper in, breathless, grubby and excited followed by their father who is a bit slower.*)

Mother M: Just look at you all. Whatever have you been doing to get so dirty?

Mouse 1: Well, we met a Bumble Bee. Such a show off.

Mouse 2: She was flying and singing just like this.

(*All children make loud buzzing noise.*)

Mouse 3: And she flew from flower to flower.

(*All the children start buzzing and flying around the room.*)

Mouse 4: She laughed at us mummy and said we were too fat to sit on flowers. Are we fat mummy?

Mother M: (*Puts her arms around as many children as she can.*) I shall tell that Bumble Bee off when I see her. None of you are fat just nicely rounded.

Mouse 5:	And she said she could dance but all she did was waggle her bum/bottom like this (*Demonstrates Father mouse laughs then coughs when mother mouse scowls at him.*)
Mouse 6:	We made good friends with the twin frogs.
Mouse 7:	They made us laugh so much. They kept jumping up high like this. (*He starts to hop like a frog — then the others join in.*)
Mouse 8:	We tried and tried to copy them. I can nearly do it. Let's show you. (*All the children Play leap frog.*)
Mouse 1:	They don't say much, They just keep saying Rabbit Rabbit Rabbit. (*All children copy and Croak out Rabbit Rabbit etc.*)
Father M:	Stop! Stop! Good gracious. What a racket.
Mouse 2:	A caterpillar came creeping past, just kept munching away.
Mouse 3:	He had a million legs and walked so strangely just like this. (*All children walk on hands and feet arching their backs as they go forward.*)
Mouse 4:	I really really loved him. He was so plump and furry.
Mouse 5:	When a butterfly came gliding by he said she was his mother.
Mouse 6:	I found that strange too. She was so beautiful and very gentle.
Mouse 7:	We could see all her lovely colours. Flying so slowly just like this (*Starts slow wing movements with arms then others do the same flying quietly around the stage sometimes low and. then higher.*)
Mother M:	You're making me dizzy trying to watch you all.
Mouse 8:	Well I didn't believe him.
Mouse 1:	Nor did I.

Mouse 2:	She kept telling him to eat his greens and not to waste time talking to those dirty little creatures.
Mouse 3:	Did she mean us? (*All the children look at each other and then nodded.*)
Mouse 4:	(*Sharply.*) Of course she meant us. Did you see anyone else around?
	(*Mouse 1 is a bit upset and to change the atmosphere.*)
Mouse 5:	Guess what else we saw? (*Breathlessly.*) A WORM.
Mouse 6:	She didn't stay long she was very afraid.
Mouse 7:	She was afraid a bird would see her and eat her.
Mouse 8:	So she wriggled away as fast as she could. Shall we show you how? (*All lie on the floor and wriggle from side to side as they move forward.*)
Father M:	That explains why you are all so mucky.
Mother M:	Clean yourselves up now good boys and girls. Then its off to bed.
Father Mouse:	Two Legs has some fine cheese in her kitchen and if you're good you shall have some for breakfast.
	(*All the children sit and frantically clean themselves using back of hand to brush their faces and bodies before lying down and sleeping*).

for nine year olds

[Bracknell]* Has Talent

Characters

Judge 1
Judge 2
Judge 3
Contestant 1 Charlie
Jugglers Judy and Macey
Singer Tina
Comedienne Perry
Audience - other contestants

Running Time

15 -20 minutes

* insert town name

Setting

On a stage with judges seated round a table.
At the side are seated the wannabes.

Three judges sit waiting for wanabee's who can be heard squabbling about who goes first. Judges sighing and waiting. The group of wanabees act as the audience for the proposed auditions.

Judge 1:   (*Irritably.*) Can we make a start please? (*A boy steps forward holding a toy animal.*)

Judge 2:   (*Gently.*) What's your name dear?

Contestant 1: (*Whispers.*) Charlie.

Judge 1:   (*Mutters*) For Heaven's sake!

Judge 2:   Speak up dear.

Charlie: (*A little louder.*) Charlie.

Judge 3:   (*Points to toy.*) Is that your lucky mascot child?

    (*Charlie Shakes head.*)

Judge 1:   (*Mutters.*) We are going to be here all night at this rate. (*Louder to contestant.*) So, young man how are you going to entertain us this evening?

Charlie: (*Shyly.*) I'm a ventriloquist and this is my friend Fredericka who will tell you a story. (*The judges sit up and show interest.*)

Judge 3:   Perhaps you'd like to begin and show us what you can do.

Charlie: (*Places the toy in his arms to manipulate it then in a loud clear confident voice begins to speak but his lips can be seen to be moving.*)

Fredericka: (*Loud, brash, very cocky.*) Hi everybody. I'm Fredericka. (*Toy is turned to Con. 1.*) 'Ere, Charlie just look at them, miserable looking lot aren't they? (*Charlie nods.*) Am I really going to tell them a story?

Charlie: (*Quiet voice.*) Do your best Fredericka, for me.

Fred.   All right my darling, I will. (*Pause while toy adjusted.*) Now then, 'cos Charlie's shy, I do all the talking understand, if we win, it'll be because of me right.

Judge 2:	I'd like to hear your story please Fredericka.
Judge 1:	Just get on with it. (*Other judges nudge him to shut up.*)
Fred:	That's it. If you're going to talk to me and Charlie like that I ain't going to bother. Goodnight. (*Audience clap as Charlie shuffles off and the Judges look at each other gob smacked, then vote NO*)
Judge 3:	Well, that's not a very good start is it?
Judge 1:	I wish I wasn't here frankly.
Judge 2:	You can't expect all the contestants to be of West End standard. Give them a chance.
Judge 3:	She's right, this might be their only chance to make good.
Judge 1:	All right, all right. I get the message (*Shouts.*) Next, and hurry up about it. (*Two sisters arrive on stage.*)
Judge 2	Good evening girls. Can you give us your names please
Both:	(*Together.*) Judy, Macey. (*They look at each other and laugh embarrassed.*)
Judy:	I'm Judy and this is Macey.
Judge 3:	Tell us Macey what are you going to do for us this evening?
Macey:	We are going to juggle for you.
Judy:	(*Gives a big smile.*) And we are really really good at it.
Judge 1:	(*Sarcastically.*) Well, let's begin then shall we … please!
	(*The girls do their best with three balls then change to using two balls but just can't manage to juggle.*)
Macey:	(*Gritting her teeth.*) You idiot! You keep dropping them.

	(The following dialogue is breathless as the girls continue their inept juggling.)
Judy:	You said it would be easy. You know I've never done juggling before.
Macey:	Well I thought you might try for my sake. Mum will be so proud of us when we win.
Judy:	More likely to ground us for being out so late.
Judge 1:	Fine! Fine! Thank you very much.
	(Judges and audience clap half heartedly, shake their heads and vote NO. The girls leave in tears thumping each other.)
Judge 3:	*(Looks at a paper in front of her.)* Who's next I wonder? *(Calls out.)* Come along the next person please.
Judge 2:	Will you give us your name dear?
Girl:	My name is Britney Spears. *(Judges gasp in amazement.)*
Tina:	*(Resigned by their surprise.)* Yes, my dad's favourite singer. And yes ... *(Boldly.)* I'm going to sing for you.
Judge 1:	*(Turns to other judges.)* If she sings like Britney Spears, I'll eat my hat, on the other hand if she does sing like the real thing I'll sign her up straight away. *(Turns to Tina.)* You sing unaccompanied?
Tina:	What do you mean?
Judge 2:	He means dear, who will play the music for you?
Tina:	*(Gruffly.)* I manage by meself. Always have.
Judge 1:	*(Sighs.)* This is truly going to be too good to be true.
Judge 3:	When you're ready Britney.
	(Tina clasps her hands together and holds them up to her chest and begins to sing, dreadfully, off key, forgetting her words. Judge 1 covers his ears,

	Judge 2 slides down in his chair Judge 3 sits up straight and has a fixed bright smile to hide her suffering.)
Judge 2:	Thank you. That was er ... unusual. Thank you.
Judge 3:	Perhaps a few more singing lessons my dear. Then come back and see us in say twenty, twenty five years.
Judge 1:	(*Sighs.*) We know you did your best dear but we must get on, so Goodnight to you Tina.
	(*Tina leaves a puzzled look on her face as she was sure she had done well. Audience clap. Judge 1 looks at his watch and is really very fed up.*)
Judge 1:	Any more ... er acts? Anything worth staying on for? I've really had enough and to be honest ... well Bracknell* talent? I'd find more with the penguins at the south pole.
Judge 3:	(*Shuffles some papers and frowns.*) I believe there is one more. A ... um ... Perry Johnson. (*Calls out.*) Perry Johnson please.
Judge 2:	(*A small person with a wide smile bounces onto the stage.*) You are Perry Johnson?
Perry:	(*Nods, does exaggerated bow does a little dance and grins.*) That's me folks. Perry Johnson the very person you've been waiting for.
Judge 1:	(*Sits up straighter and shows an interest*) And what is it, Perry you think you are going to enter-tain us with?
Perry:	Ah, your honour, (*Gives a bow.*) I intend to make you laugh. (*Judges look at each other and smile indulgently at Perry.*) Yes, I see already you are half way there.
Judge 2:	So what is it you want to be Perry?
Perry:	A comedian your lordship, the best there is. (*He bows to Judge.*)

Judge 1:	Well get on with it. (*Sighs as convinced this is another duff act.*)
Perry:	What's the difference between a witch and the letters M, A, K, E?
	(*Pause, no one answers.*) One makes spells and the other spells make.
	(*Judges smile, and audience cheer.*)
Perry:	(*Walks a few steps away then returns.*) Knock, knock.
Audience:	Who's there?
Perry:	Ivor
Audience:	Ivor who?
Perry:	Ivor good mind not to tell you. (*Audience cheers.*)
	What were your school days like? I remember one day the teacher said to me, 'Why are you late, Perry?' and I told her because of a sign down the road. and she asked, 'What did the sign have to do with your being late?' and I answered, 'The sign said, "School Ahead, Go Slow!"'
Judge 1:	(*Beaming.*) At last! This one's got a bit of talent.
Judge 2:	Certainly entertaining me.
Perry:	(*Wags his finger at judges.*) Let me tell you about a little girl who said to her mother, 'Mummy, today in school I was punished for something that I didn't do.' The mother was very angry, 'But that's terrible! I'm going to have a talk with your teacher about this, what was it that you didn't do?' and the little girl replied, 'My homework.'
	(*Audience cheers, Perry bows.*)
Perry:	Knock knock.
Audience:	Who's there?
Perry:	Conan.
Audience:	Conan who?

Perry	Conan the cob! (*Laughter and cheers from every-one. Judges enjoying themselves. Perry turns to them.*) Here's a computer joke. Adults seem afraid of computers but here goes.
	Why did the computer sneeze? (*Mutterings among the audience and Judges.*) Want to know? (*All call out YES Perry grins.*) Because ... (*Long pause.*) because it had a virus! (*Lots of laughter.*)
	Knock, knock ... (*Judge 2 interrupts.*)
Judge 3:	Thank you Perry, you've certainly made us smile this evening. Well done.
	(*The judges confer for a few moments.*)
Judge 1:	Thank you everyone for taking the trouble to come here this evening. We have seen and heard some ... um, er ... different acts but I think you will agree with the judges that without a doubt Perry was the most enjoyable. So hands together every-one for Perry Johnson. I am sure we are going to hear more of him in the future.
	(*Clapping all round.*)

for nine year olds

The Aliens

Characters

Ruby

Jo

Kerry

Cathy

Guest 1

Guest 2

Guest 3

Guest 4

Guest 5

Guest 6

Mother

Running Time

15 minutes

Setting

Outdoor picnic area or similar.

Four children in one group Ruby, Jo, Kerry and Cathy lying on their stomachs chins in hands. Second group on birthday picnic outing unlimited number.

Ruby: Look at them, wished they'd asked us to their picnic.

Jo: Well, they don't know us yet. We only moved into our new house yesterday.

Kerry: But it would have been nice to have been asked. They could get to know us then.

Cathy: Oh, I don't care. (*All look wistfully at picnic group playing a game.*)

Ruby: (*Whispers longingly.*) Just look at all that food.

Jo: I'm starving. (*All go on watching other group who now sit down to eat.*)

Kerry: (*Long pause then Kerry sits up quickly, excited.*) Listen! I've got a brilliant idea!

Ruby: No, Kerry. No. Every time you have a brilliant idea we get into trouble.

Kerry: You'll like it I promise and I can't see why it should get us into bother.

Cathy: Ruby's right we …

Kerry: Oh yes, Ruby's always right but this time you'll love it.

Jo: O.K., tell us this wonderful idea of yours and we'll put it to the vote.

Kerry: (*Hugging her knees and all the others sit up.*) I thought … (*Thinks for a moment.*) I thought we could pretend to be aliens from another planet investigating the planet earth!

Ruby: But we're already humans and we're already here.

Kerry: Pretend, know what that means? Be someone else for a change.

Jo: And then what?

Kerry: We can go up to them, and ask them questions, tell them things about where we've come from then they'd have to talk to us.

Ruby: But we come from Tilehurst*. [Local vicinity]

Cathy: (*Rolls her eyes, shrugs her shoulders.*) Tell her someone.

Jo: I think it's a good idea. It's a good idea, come on let's do it. (*They approach the other group.*)

Kerry: (*Whispers to the other three.*) Let me start the talking. (*Turns to the picnic group.*) Hello, who are you? (*The picnic group stare at the four newcomers.*)

Guest 1:   (*Surprised.*) Where did you come from?

Kerry: We've come from Stulthree.

Guest 2:   Never heard of it.

Kerry: It's a planet. It's hidden behind your moon.

Guest 3:   (*Shouting excitedly.*) They're aliens.

            (*The 'aliens' look pleased.*)

Guest 4 & 5: (*Absolutely awed.*) Aliens.

Guest 6:   Wait till I tell my brother, boy will he be mad he missed you.

Guest 1:   So how come you know how to speak our language.

Kerry: We have been listening to your people for a long time and it is so easy to learn.

Guest 2:   So, why aren't you wearing funny clothes like we see on pictures of the strange creatures on Mars?

Jo: We're far cleverer than they are. All we do is 'think' ourselves like you

Guest 4:	What do you want from us anyway? We're having a birthday party for invited people only so I think you ought to go away now.
Guest 3:	Oh! I love aliens. Let them stay. Perhaps they'll tell us about their planet.
Ruby:	(*Innocently.*) Oh, it's earth really. (*Cathy pinches her and scowls.*) Ouch! I mean it's just like earth really.
Guest 5:	Earth is the best place to be. I bet you don't ... (*Interrupted.*)
Jo:	What is a birthday party?
Guest 1:	It's my birthday today. It means ten years ago I came into the world. So I am having a party
Cathy:	(*Pretending ignorance.*) The world? What is that?
Guest 5:	It's another name for the earth planet.
Cathy:	And 'a party' is ...?
Guest 1:	We all play games and have lovely lovely food.
Jo:	(*Trying hard not to look longingly at the food.*) Food? What is that?
Guest 2:	We eat it. Here try some. (*She hands Jo a cake and the other three aliens put out their hands and eat making faces of enjoyment.*)
Ruby:	Oh, just so so wonderful.
Guest 3:	Try this. (*Hands out a dish of jelly, the other aliens put out their hands.*)
Jo:	(*Pokes at a pile of sandwiches.*) What are these?
Guest 4:	Sandwiches, with strawberry jam in. Try one. (*The aliens gradually eat all the food.*)
Guest 6:	(*Begins to protest.*) But you've eaten everything. There's nothing left for me or my friends.
Ruby:	Please don't cry. You can come to my party next month. I'll be nine.
Guest 5:	(*Rudely.*) I don't believe you're aliens at all.

Guest 1:	No nor do I. If you're as clever as you say just fill up the plates with food again.
Guest 4:	I want to know how you got here. Is there a space-ship hidden somewhere? Let's go and see it.
Kerry:	(*Getting flustered, waves her arms about and looks around her.*) Er ... er ... we can't make your food and er ... I ...
Ruby:	We fell through a hole in the sky. (*The picnic children laugh, they obviously don't believe her.*)
Guest 4:	(*Sadly.*) So there's no spaceship then. I always wanted to go inside one.
Jo:	I feel a bit sick
Ruby:	And I've got an awful tummy ache.
Kerry:	It must be the food of these earth people.
Guest 6:	Don't you dare say that. My mum made every bit of that food.
	(*Suddenly a frantic voice is heard calling.*)
Mother:	Kerry, Jo, Cathy, Ruby where are you? (*The aliens begin to hurry away from the picnic but their mother catches them.*) There you are. What have you been up to?
Guest 3:	Are you their mother? (*Mother looks at all the children then nods.*)
Guest 5:	And you are really a human being?
Mother:	(*Laughs.*) Of course did you think I came from out of space or something?
	(*The picnic children look very cross at the aliens.*)
Mother:	What's been going on here? (*Pause.*) Ruby? (*Pause.*) Kerry? I see all the food has gone. Did these naughty ones eat it all?
	(*All the guests nod.*)
Guest 2:	They said they were from out of space.

Guest 4: So there really is no spaceship? (*Mother shakes her head.*)

Mother: I tell you what. Tomorrow why don't you all come round to our house, just there down the road, and have a housewarming party with us.

Kerry: We could make it a space theme party.

Mother: That's enough Kerry. You've all done enough about space for one day.

Ruby: Can we go home now. I feel so poorly with my tummy ache.

Guest 1: (*Turns to the picnic group.*) How about it? Shall we go tomorrow

(*They all nod.*)

Mother: Good, good. I'll make everyone's favourite food and you can all become good friends. Goodbye. (*They leave and the others wave a friendly goodbye.*)

for twelve year olds

Some Detective Work

Characters

Mia

Paula

Daisy

Becca

Flora

Hannah

Amber

Running Time

10-15 minutes

Setting

Room with a few piece of furniture.
A glass with dregs of fruit drink, sweet papers, a tissue, etc.
lying around, and a school bag and books on the table.

A group of children in a room with a few piece of furniture. There is a glass with dregs of fruit drink, sweet papers, a tissue, etc. lying around, and a school bag and books on the table.

Mia: (*Searching around the room frantically.*) Someone's stolen my phone.

Paula: (*Crossly.*) Don't say that. Say something like someone's borrowed my phone without asking, but stealing is a bit unkind especially as we're all friends.

Mia: I don't care! I just want my phone back. My dad will kill me if it's gone missing.

Daisy: Let's all have a good search round, it must be somewhere.

(*All begin rushing around moving things and searching.*)

Mia: Has anyone found it yet?

(*Murmuring and shaking heads. Mia begins to cry. Someone consoles her and the others give up hunting. There is a long pause as no one knows what to do now.*)

Becca: Well, it's no good just standing around. If one of us has taken it, it should be easy to find out who.

Flora: How, for goodness' sake.

Becca: We shall become detectives!

Hannah: Like on the telly?

Becca: Exactly like real detectives. (*Everyone brightens up and smile at each other.*)

Amber: So really we have to look for clues.

Becca: Yes, that's it. Come on let's get started. See what we can find.

Daisy:	You have to be very careful so you don't spoil the evidence.
Flora:	What are we looking for?
Becca:	Anything that we can't explain. Put anything you find on the table. Now let's get started.
	(*They all search very carefully on the furniture and floor picking up whatever they find including sweet wrappers, an elastic hair band paper tissue etc.*)
Hannah:	I think we've just about got everything now.
Amber:	(*Sits down exhausted.*) Gosh, I'm tired out.
Becca:	So, let's see what we've got. (*Picks up a sweet wrapper.*) Who's got sweets in their pocket?
	(*A chorus of 'Not me, Not me' from others.*)
Paula:	I saw Daisy chewing just a while ago.
Daisy:	(*Indignant.*) Well, that doesn't mean I took the phone.
Becca:	That's only the first clue. Look what's this? (*Picks up tissue.*)
Flora:	Someone has got a cold I'll bet. (*Hannah sniffs loudly then sneezes and everyone turns to look at her.*)
Hannah:	Don't look at me! I've got hay fever from all the dust you've been stirring up.
Amber:	It could be you. You're the only one who hasn't got a mobile phone yet. You told me you was getting one for your birthday.
Hannah:	(*Angrily.*) Are you accusing me Amber Wilson? 'Cos it could be you. You've got purple drink marks all round your mouth and the glass is on the table where the phone is supposed to be.
Daisy:	Oh! And how do you know the phone was on the table, I wonder.

Mia:	I thought that is where I put it. I can't remember now but I daren't go home without it. I'll be grounded forever, honest I will.
Paula:	What if we all turn our backs and whoever has got it sneaks across and puts it back on the table. That way no one will ever know who er ... borrowed it.
Flora:	I'd say that's a very good idea. Shall we try it? (*They all nod turn their backs so they can't see each other and stand waiting for a long time.*)
Hannah:	(*Plaintively.*) Do you think we've waited long enough now?
Amber:	Let's all turn round when I say 5. (*Counts slowly.*) One, two, three, four, five.
	(*All turn round and look at the empty table.*)
Mia:	(*Bursts into tears.*) I was hoping it would be there. Please whoever has got it give it to me. I won't ever tell the others. Please, please. (*Continues sobbing.*)
Paula:	I've been thinking. It must be someone who hasn't already got a phone, so hands up those who haven't got one.
	(*Daisy and Hannah put up their hands.*)
Amber:	(*Excited.*) See! And the clues we found matches them. (*Daisy begins to cry.*)
Hannah:	You're all so unfair. I tell you it isn't me.
Daisy:	(*Tearfully.*) And it isn't me. (*Daisy and Hannah go across to each other and link arms to support each other.*)
Becca:	That means the rest of us have. (*Takes out her own phone, looks at it thoughtfully for a short while.*) I have an idea.
Flora:	Well your last one wasn't very good was it? I mean it got us nowhere.
Becca:	Mia, what's your number.

Mia:	It's (*Gets out a scrap of paper and reads.*) 077653941
Becca:	0, seven, seven, six, five, three nine, four, one. (*Pause, then a phone is heard. Everyone looks around surprised and Paula goes over and looks under the pile of books.*)
Paula:	(*Smugly.*) Look what I've found!
Mia:	(*Excited.*) Oh! thank you, thank you, thank you!
Amber:	Problem solved, but how come we didn't find it before?
Becca:	Because we all thought that was the last place where the phone had been left so non of us bothered to look.
Mia:	I'm sorry. It's my fault. I got all those books from the library to do my homework on Alexander Bell and I must have put them on top of my phone.
Flora:	(*Squealing.*) Alexander Bell! But he invented the telephone.
	(*Everyone laughs happily.*)

for fourteen — sixteen year olds

A Hasty Judgement

Characters

Samantha

Joe

Emily

Sarah

Tiffany

Amy

Jenna

Rachel

Running Time

15-20 minutes

Setting

School common room.

Group of girls chatting, laughing, sharing sweets etc a general get together school common room. Samantha accompanied by her brother Joe hurries to join them.

Samantha: Hiya everyone.

(*Everyone turns their back on her, but surreptitiously keep glancing at Joe who is uncomfortable with the attention.*)

Joe: (*Moving away quickly from the crowd.*) I'm off Sam, see you at home.

Sam: (*Quietly.*) Bye, Joe. (*Turns to the group.*) What's up? What have I done to upset you lot?

Emily: Remember girls, we are not going to speak to … this snobby pig ever again.

Sam: (*Shocked.*) But what …

Sarah: (*Slyly.*) What did you say this ex friend of yours did Tiffany?

Sam: (*Turns to Tiffany.*) Tiff, Tiff? What have I ever …

Tiffany: Look, she's trying to talk to me. Can't she take a hint.

Amy: So, Tif, what exactly did she do? (*They all get closer to TIF. Making sure SAM is left alone.*)

Tif:. As I said before, I was walking along the High Street this morning and I saw HER coming towards me with her mother and when I said 'Hello', well her nose went up in the air and she ignored me completely. (*Pretends to cry and the girls say various soothing words.*) And I was her best friend.

Sam: But I never saw you. I didn't have my glasses on.

Tif: She could have said at least hello back.

Sam: But it is so noisy in the High Street and mother was …

Jenna: We're agreed then. That person is no longer in our group.

(All nod in agreement.)

Sarah: Shame in a way. *(All glare at her. SARAH stutters.)* I mean, er I mean … Well girls just look at her brother. Really a dishy guy.

Amy: *(Dreamily.)* Joe! Yes, you've got a point. I suppose we could …

Tif: No we couldn't. It would mean having to talk to HER politely If he dates one of us.

Sam: He says he rather fancies …

(They all look at SAM expectantly. SAM shrugs her shoulders.)

Sarah: One thing I will miss not speaking to you know who, well she's pretty good at helping me with my maths homework.

Emily: She's nothing but a swot and a snob.

Jenna: And a teacher's pet. Did you notice last week Miss Digsby give her a big smile and a grade A for that crappy essay.

(All nod. SAM moves away from them, dejected and feels alone, weeping quietly she takes out her book and pretends to read.)

Amy: I bet she's swotting up now. Thinks she's good enough for college. *(Marches across to SAM and snatches book which she waves at the others.)* See, I was right. She's reading *(Pause.)* She's reading Shakespeare! *(She throws book on to the floor.)*

Sarah: So what? If she goes to college we won't have to look at her ugly face again.

Jenna: That's something I can't understand. I mean, Joe. Just look at him so good looking and FRIENDLY and her *(Goes across and pokes SAM hard.)* so gross!

Emily:	When that happens in families my mother says someone's been playing around. (*Shocked faces all round and then giggles.*)
Sam:	You evil people. How dare you speak like that about my family.
The Group:	(*Shouting.*) Shut up, slut.
Amy:	Yes, slut. You'll end up just like your mother.
	(*As the group leaves laughing, they jostle and push and point at* SAM*'s obvious discomfort.* SAM *sits for a short time undecided what to do.*)
Sam:	I'm not a snob. I'm not a snob. (*Pause.*) I wish they'd listened to me I just didn't see Tiffany. I wouldn't do that to her. (*Mumbles.*) or any of them. (*Strides about angrily.*) It's not fair. (*She slumps into a chair and tries to read but keeps daydreaming and sighing. The door opens and* RACHEL *enters.*)
Sam:	(*Brightening up.*) Oh! Hello Rachel. (RACHEL *ignores her and searches for her bag.*) Have you lost something?
Rachel:	Yes, my bag it's got my ... (*Claps her hand to her mouth.*) Oh, I'm not allowed to talk to you.
Sam:	Yes you can.
Rachel:	Can't.
Sam:	But you are!
Rachel:	Tiffany says we are not to.
Sam:	(*Laughing.*) But she's not here.
Rachel:	You won't tell her will you that I have? Now I will not speak to you again, ever. I just forgot. (SAM *is crestfallen and tries to ignore Rachel picks up her book but she keeps glancing up to see what she is doing.*)
Rachel:	(*Muttering to herself.*) It's here somewhere I know it is. (*Keeps searching then trips over. Pause. Then*

she begins to moan in pain.) Umm, Sam. Samantha. (*Sam ignores her.*) Sam, please. (SAM *looks up.*)

Sam: You're not allowed to speak to me remember?

Rachel: I know, but I think I've broken my ankle.

Sam: (*Snaps.*) Well, you'd better call Tiffany then. You've got a mobile?

Rachel: (*Crying now in pain.*) Help me Sam, please. (SAM *goes over to her and bends over her and touches ankle.*) Ow! Ow!

Sam: Oh, Rach, I think you're right, and your arm. Is that broken too?

Rachel: (*Painfully.*) No, I don't think so, my wrist hurts though. What shall we do?

Sam: Lend me your phone and I'll get an ambulance, I think you'll have to go to A & E for proper help.

Rachel: Don't leave me Samantha. I don't want to be alone.

Sam: (*Begins tapping out on phone.*) As if I would, we've been friends since primary school that counts for something doesn't it! (*Talks into phone.*) Tilehurst* High School. (*Pause.*) Samantha Bell. (*Pause.*) My friend has fallen over and has hurt her ankle and wrist. (*Pause.*) Broken? We think so. (*Pause.*) Thank you. (*Kneels beside* RACHEL.) Now, I'm not going to touch you but here's my coat. I've rolled it into a cushion for you to lean on.

Rachel: (*Tearfully.*) Thank you. Will they be long?

Sam: Ten minutes is what they thought. (*Sound of ambulance and all the group rush back in.*)

Tif: (*Shrieking.*) Get away from her.

Rachel: Tif, it's al ...

Emily: What's happened?

Amy: You alright Rachel? Has she done this to you?

Sarah: Wouldn't put it past her, knowing what she's like.

Rachel: (*Raising herself up onto her good elbow.*) Shut up all of you if it wasn't for Sam, I could have been lying here for hours. She's looked after me, made me a pillow, got the ambulance. Been really kind to me. So ... leave her alone, and another thing Tif. I shall speak to her whenever I like.

Amy: (*Goes across to* SAM.) Is this true? You really helped her after all the things we've said about you. (SAM *nods.*) Well, she's my friend too and I shall always speak to you Sam. (*They embrace.*)

Tif: I'm sorry Sam, I must have got it all wrong. You were so busy talking to your mother I'm sure now that you didn't see. (*She puts out her hand towards* SAM.) Friends?

Sam: (*Beams delightedly and nods.*) Of course.

            (*The rest of the group all go across and embrace her.*)

The group: Sorry Sam.

Sam: Tell you what, when Rachel gets back, shall we all go to McDonalds?

Sarah: (*Wistfully.*) Do you think Joe might come?

Sam: Not likely! He hardly speaks to me and I bet you lot would make him die of embarrassment. Anyway, he's crazy about football.

Sarah: (*Brightly.*) So am I.

Tif: Since when?

Sarah: Since (*Hesitates.*) Since now!

The group: (*Except* SAM *shouting above each other.*) And me!

Sam: (*Laughing.*) I'll tell him, shall I? I'll tell him there's a girls' football team ready to take him on. Anyway , come on, I think you ought to treat me to a Big Mac.

            (*They leave the stage laughing and hugging.*)

Plays by Beatrice

A Certain Monday
Connie's Lovely Boy
From Commoner to Coronet
Governed by Magpies
In Less than Ten Minutes
Plays for Young Actors

Books by Beatrice

Children's
The Adventures of Rhys:
○ Training a Greyhound
○ Urgent! Pocket Money Required
○ Disasters and Delights of Family Celebrations
○ The Sometimes Society
Towpath Tale series
○ Towing Path Tales
○ More Towing Path Tales
○ A Particular Year
Adult
The man from the North East
Elusive Destiny

www.ingramcontent.com/pod-product-compliance
Lightning Source LLC
LaVergne TN
LVHW051712080426
835511LV00017B/2882